My Home

Story by Jillian Cutting

I went into the kitchen.
My mom was there!

I went into the bathroom.
My dad was there!

I went into the living room.
My brother was there!

4

I went into the dining room.
My sister was there!

I went into the TV room.
My dog was there!

I went into the bedroom

I was there!